Teacher

Thank You for...

y mentor.

You showed me how to

_____

_____

_____

_____

_____

_____

_____

_____

Thanks

for showing me what can b

...complished with patience.

Here's what I have accomplished

_____

_____

_____

_____

_____

_____

_____

_____

ring and dedication.

This was visible when you

_____

_____

_____

_____

_____

_____

_____

_____

Thank You
for making

...laughter a part of each day.

I giggle when I recall

_____

_____

_____

_____

_____

_____

_____

_____

Thank You
for caring ho...

I spent my day.

My favorite part of a day in your classroom was

_____

_____

_____

_____

_____

_____

_____

_____

Thank You
for being o

he cutting edge.

You made learning new and exciting with

_____

_____

_____

_____

_____

_____

_____

me when I struggled.

Remember the time I had difficulty with

_____

_____

_____

_____

_____

_____

_____

_____

Thanks for
your creativity

the learning process.

You made learning fun when

_____

_____

_____

_____

_____

_____

_____

_____

Thanks
for showing me that

mall steps are all it takes.

I'll never forget how you taught me to

_____

_____

_____

_____

_____

_____

_____

_____

an overcome fear.

When I was uncertain you

_____

_____

_____

_____

_____

_____

_____

_____

Thanks
for sharing with me you

houghts on life.

${Y}$ou have an interesting way of

_____

_____

_____

_____

_____

_____

_____

_____

...be mediocre.

You are a star when it comes to

_____

_____

_____

_____

_____

_____

_____

_____

my creativity.

My individuality is important and thanks to you I have

_____

_____

_____

_____

_____

_____

_____

_____

You have

taught me th

importance of never giving up.

With your help I have successfully

_____

_____

_____

_____

_____

_____

_____

_____

Thank You for making

lassroom discussions exciting.

A subject that was so interesting was

_____

_____

_____

_____

_____

_____

_____

_____

to the many books I read.

I so enjoyed this particular book because

_____

_____

_____

_____

_____

_____

_____

_____

ithout your energetic attitude.

Your positive attitude really rubbed off on me when

_____

_____

_____

_____

_____

_____

_____

_____

...indow to the world.

With you as my teacher I found out about

_____

_____

_____

_____

_____

_____

_____

Thanks
for turning an averag

...day into a day of fun.

You really got me to participate when you

_____

_____

_____

_____

_____

_____

_____

_____

...to a real life adventure.

I will never forget the day that you

_____

_____

_____

_____

_____

_____

_____

_____

I am so grateful
for the many gifts yo

rought into the classroom.

Here are three of your gifts that made a difference in my life

_____

_____

_____

_____

_____

_____

_____

_____

Thank You

for encouraging

...e to explore new goals.

The doors you opened changed my outlook on

_____

_____

_____

_____

_____

_____

_____

hen I needed to talk.

On one particular occasion you helped me to understand

_____

_____

_____

_____

_____

_____

_____

_____

Thanks
for creating days tha

I won't forget.

The subjects that were so interesting were

_____

_____

_____

_____

_____

_____

_____

Thanks
for being a teacher wh

es the world in new ways.

Here is one subject that you made me see differently

_____

_____

_____

_____

_____

_____

_____

_____

Thank You

for teaching

e the power of discovery.

You had a knack for showing me the magic in

_____

_____

_____

_____

_____

_____

_____

_____

Thanks to you

creativity became

weekly part of my life.

My creativity has enhanced my outlook on

_____

_____

_____

_____

_____

_____

_____

_____

nto the learning process.

I had no idea that

_____

_____

_____

_____

_____

_____

_____

_____

mbrace new possibilities.

Something new I tried because of you is

_____

_____

_____

_____

_____

_____

_____

_____

There were

sunny day

nd cloudy days.

Thanks for showing me how to put one foot in front of the other on a daily basis.

_____

_____

_____

_____

_____

_____

_____

_____

There's only one you.
It has been a priviley

…be a part of your life.

Thank you.

_____

_____

_____

_____

_____

_____

_____

_____

© 2004 Havoc Publishing
San Diego, California
U.S.A.

Text by Maureen Webster

ISBN 0-7416-1312-3

www.havocpub.com

Made in Korea